The life cycle of a
Honeybee

Ruth Thomson

WAYLAND

First published in 2006 by Wayland
an imprint of Hachette Children's Books

British Library Cataloguing in Publication Data
Thomson, Ruth
  The life cycle of a honeybee. - (Learning About Life Cycles)
  I. Honeybee - Life cycles - Juvenile literature
I Title
571.8'15799

Editor: Victoria Brooker
Designer: Simon Morse
Senior Design Manager: Rosamund Saunders

Printed and bound in China

Hachette Children's Books
A division of Hodder Headline Limited
338 Euston Road, London NW1 3BH

Photographs: Page 1, 8 and cover (bottom) Martin
Gabriel/naturepl.com; 2 and 7 (bottom), 6, cover (top) 9 and 23
(top left), 10, 12 and cover (middle) and 23 (top right), 13 and 23
(bottom right), 15 Kim Taylor/naturepl.com; 4-5 Jeff Foote/
naturepl.com; 7 (top) Frank Greenaway © Dorling
Kindersley /dkimages; 7 (middle) Getty Images; 11
Oxford Scientific Films; 14, 18, 19, 20 John B Free/
naturepl.com; 16 and cover main image © Gallo
Images/CORBIS; 17 Meul/ARCO/naturepl.com; 21
Sinclair Stammers/Science Photo Library; 22
and 23 (bottom left) Scott Camazine/Alamy

ISBN-13: 9780750248617
ISBN-10: 0750248610

Contents

Honeybees live here

Thousands of honeybees live together in a honeycomb nest, made of six-sided **wax cells**.

5

What is a honeybee?

A honeybee is an insect with six legs, three parts to its body and two feelers. Unlike most insects, it has a sting, which it uses for **defence**.

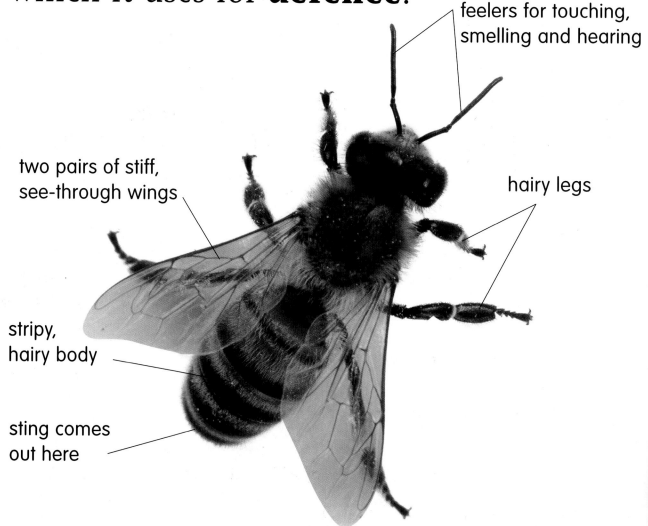

feelers for touching, smelling and hearing

two pairs of stiff, see-through wings

hairy legs

stripy, hairy body

sting comes out here

Three kinds of honeybee live in a nest.

There is one queen. ▶
She is the biggest bee.

◀ There are hundreds
of males called drones.

There are thousands
of small females
called workers. ▶

Queen bee

The queen bee stays in the nest
all the time. She is always surrounded
by worker bees who feed her.
Her only job is to lay eggs.

She lays a tiny egg in every empty **cell**. Sometimes, she lays up to a thousand eggs a day.

Grub

After three days, each egg hatches into a blind, legless **grub**. At first, it feeds on rich milky food called **royal jelly** and grows very fast.

Three days later, workers give
the grub a mixture of **pollen** and
honey to eat instead. At six days old,
the grub is so fat that it fills its **cell**.

Pupa

The **grub** stops feeding. Workers put a **wax** lid on its **cell**. The grub spins silk around itself and becomes a **pupa**. Day by day, its body changes.

pupa

wax lid

12

Almost two weeks later, the fully-grown bee bites off the wax lid and crawls out of its cell. Workers greet it with their feelers.

1 day

Worker bees

New worker bees start work straightaway.
They clean empty **cells** ready for eggs.
Next, they feed the new **grubs**.

1-10
days

2
weeks

Then workers become builders
and make new cells. Some guard
the honeycomb nest and fight
insects that want to steal honey.

Food collectors

The workers start sucking **nectar** from flowers and storing it inside their body. Back at the nest, the bees put the nectar into **cells**. It changes into honey.

The bees also collect a yellow dust called **pollen** from flowers. They carry the pollen back to the nest in hollows called pollen baskets on their back legs.

3-5 weeks

A new queen

When a new queen is needed, workers build larger **cells** for them. They feed the **grubs** only on **royal jelly**.

There can be only one new queen.
The first to come out stings the others
to death in their cells. If two come out
at once, they fight until one is killed.

Moving and mating

The old queen and thousands of workers fly out of the nest in a great cloud. They **swarm** around trees looking for a new home.

The new queen flies out of the nest.
The drones chase after her. One drone
mates with her. After mating, the drone
dies. The queen returns to the nest.

Back to the nest

In the nest, the young queen starts
her lifelong job of laying eggs.
These will become new honeybees.

Honeybee life cycle

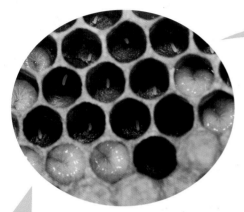

Eggs
The queen lays eggs in **cells**. After 3 days, a **grub** hatches.

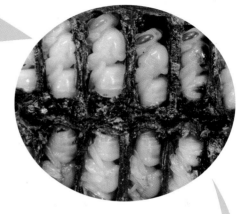

Pupa
After 6 days, the grub becomes a **pupa**.

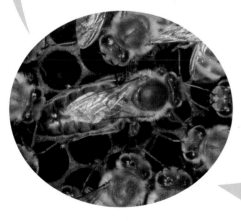

Queen bee
The queen bee leaves to make a new nest and a new queen bee takes over.

Bees
After 12 days, a new worker bee comes out of its cell.

Glossary

cell a small chamber

defence protection against attack

grub the soft, young stage of insects such as bees

mate when a male and female join together to produce young

nectar the sweet liquid that bees collect from flowers

pollen the yellow powder in flowers

pupa the form that an insect takes when it changes from a grub to an adult

royal jelly a rich creamy food for bee grubs, especially queen grubs

swarm to move in great numbers

wax a sticky material made by bees, used for making honeycomb cells

Index